Top 10 Intimacy Needs

Top 10 Intimacy Needs

Dr. David Ferguson
Dr. Don McMinn

Intimacy Press
Austin, Texas

Intimacy Press
P.O.Box 201808, Austin, Texas, 78720-1808
1-800-881-8008 Fax - 512-795-0853

ISBN - 0-9642845-0-2
Library of Congress Catalog Card Number: 94-72620

Clients' names and details of their stories have been changed, fictionalized, and intermingled to protect their identities.

CMFI - A Ministry of Hope and Healing

The Center For Marriage and Family Intimacy is a non-profit ministry which provides instruction and materials to assist individuals, churches, and other ministries in the development of a comprehensive marriage and family ministry and a ministry that encourages intimacy with God. CMFI resources include:

- *The Pursuit of Intimacy* book
- *Intimate Encounters* Workbook
- *Intimate Moments* Devotional Guide
- Topical Booklets
- Church Leader's Guide
- Leadership Audio Tapes
- Home Study Seminars
- Ministry Orientation Kit
- Songs of Intimacy Tapes and Songbooks
- Intimacy Notes

CMFI also publishes the *Marriage and Family Intimacy Newsletter* which addresses key issues regarding developing meaningful relationships with God, your spouse, children, and others. For a free 5-month gift subscription, contact the CMFI office.

Key elements in CMFI's message include our need for intimacy with both God and meaningful others, our need to "experience" biblical truth, and God's provision for both our "fallen-ness" and our "aloneness."

For more information about conferences and seminars sponsored by CMFI, or to receive a catalog of CMFI resources or a free copy of the monthly newsletter, call or write:

The Center For Marriage and Family Intimacy
P.O.Box 201808, Austin, Texas 78720-1808
1-800-881-8008   Fax - 512-795-0853

How To Use This Booklet

Top 10 Intimacy Needs is one of the *Intimacy Series* booklets produced by the Center For Marriage and Family Intimacy. The booklets deal with pertinent subjects relating to marriage, family, and the church. They are designed to be both practical and interactive and can be used in a variety of settings:

- Adult and youth Sunday school
- Discipleship groups
- Marriage and family classes
- As a supplement to counseling
- Enrichment/support groups
- Marriage staff meetings
- Family devotionals
- Personal devotionals
- Sermon material

At the end of each chapter there are: **Discussion questions, personal assessment questions**, and **suggestions for practical application**. Completing these sections will greatly enhance the reader's comprehension of the material and its potential usefulness. The material can be adopted for different lengths of study. For example, for an 8-week study, discuss one chapter and its discussion questions one week, and the following week discuss the personal assessment and practical application sections.

For a list of all booklets produced by CMFI, contact the CMFI office (information on previous page).

Chapter 1 - Needs - We All Have Them

*"And my God will meet all your **needs**..."* (Philippians 4:19).

God created you with physical, soulish, and spiritual needs.

A common denominator among all humans is the fact that we all have needs.

You have physical needs.
> Your body needs food and water.
> Your body needs sleep.
> Your body needs air.

But you're more than just a body - the intangible part of you, the real you, is your soul and spirit. And just as your body has physical needs, your soul has emotional needs, and your spirit has spiritual needs.

Physical needs are so obvious - no one would deny them; but just as real, though not as apparent, are your soulish, emotional, and intimacy needs, including:

Acceptance	Security
Approval	Respect
Encouragement	Attention
Support	Comfort
Affection	Appreciation

Spiritually you need:
> Communion with God
> Freedom from guilt and shame
> Forgiveness
> A clear conscience
> Peace
> Love

Characteristics of Needs

Needs are *cross–cultural*.

Africans have the same physical, emotional, and spiritual needs as Anglos, Orientals, and Latin Americans; needs transcend cultural differences. It doesn't matter if:

- your skin is black or yellow,
- you live in a mud hut or a brick house,
- you eat tortillas or crepes,
- you drive a car or push a rickshaw.

Needs are *the same in all generations*.

Adam, Abraham, Pilate, Tertulious, Mozart, Lincoln, Churchill, and you all share one thing in common - they, and you, all had/have needs. Needs are not a 20th century phenomenon; every person who has ever lived or will live has needs.

Needs are *life–long* and *continuous*.

Have you ever noticed that all young children share the same inherent needs. When you bring a baby home from the hospital, they exhibit a need for:

Attention - Even if their diaper is dry, they've been fed, and they've had plenty of sleep, they're likely to cry just because they want attention.

Comfort - Often, when a child falls down, he looks around to see if anyone noticed. If he doesn't see anyone, he'll "suck it up" and go on. But if he realizes that someone saw the incident, he'll cry - because he needs - comfort.

Affection - When children are around people they trust, they'll often hold their hands up, wanting to be held, embraced, and hugged. Why? They want affection. Clinical studies conducted concerning the Nazi concentration camps show that even when young children had air, food, and water - if they were not touched and given affection, they often died.

Approval - Why do children always want you to notice the picture they just drew, their "expertise" on the basketball court, or the song they just learned on the piano? It's because they have a need for approval.

Are these simply "childhood" needs which you "grow out of" with maturity? Can these needs be met once for all? If needs are legitimately met early in life, can you scratch them off the list and go on to something else?

The answer to all these questions is - No!

Adults do have the same needs as children. An octogenarian living in a nursing home has the same need for attention and comfort as a 4-year old.

And your needs must be continually met, they cannot be met "once for all." It's not as though you have an 8-ounce cup in your heart representing your need for attention, and once the cup is full, you'll not need any more. You *do* have a distinct need for attention, but like your need for air, food, or water: it must be constantly replenished.

God created us with needs so that we might exercise faith as we lovingly relate to one another.

*"The God of all comfort, **who comforts us** in all our troubles, so that **we can comfort those in any trouble** with the comfort we ourselves have received from God"* (2 Corinthians 1:4).

It's obvious that we have needs "built in" to our physical, emotional, and spiritual DNA. But the question is...Why? Why did God create us with a need for sleep? Why do we need air? And why do we all yearn for comfort, attention, and security? Do these needs represent flaws in God's design? Did He create imperfect creatures? Why did God create us with needs?

Before we answer that question, we need to realize that **we can't meet our own needs.** For instance, you can't meet your own need for comfort. The next time you have a hard day and need comforting, wrap your arms around your own neck, gently pat yourself on your back and tell yourself, "I'm so sorry you've had a hard day. Tell me all about it. I hurt for you." It just doesn't work that way.

Or how about your need for attention? Perhaps you can stare at yourself in the mirror for an hour and say things like, "How are you doing? You really look nice today. Tell me the latest news about your job. Wanna go to lunch?" But your need for attention will not be satiated.

You may be thinking, "Ah, but what about my physical needs; I can meet those myself." Oh, can you? Yes, you may be able to earn money in order to buy food, and you may be competent to cook and prepare the food, but where did that food initially come from? It was grown in the ground...and who made the seed...and who made the rain to fall, the sun to shine...where did the fertilizer come from...and the oxygen? The farmer may be able to plant seed and cultivate and harvest a crop, and we may be able to purchase and prepare food, but the source of all these good things is beyond ourselves.

So why did God create us with needs?

God created us with needs so that we might lovingly relate to Him and to one another, looking beyond ourselves for the supply.

Here's how it works:

- Everyone has needs.
- You can't meet your own needs; therefore,
- You have to look beyond yourself - to your Creator.

Your Creator may meet your needs "directly" or indirectly through relationships with meaningful others. He will also want to involve you in meeting the needs of others.

Because we all have needs, we need each other! If we didn't have needs, we'd be like computerized robots on an assembly line - doing our own thing with no regard for others.

It's like having an itch in the middle of your back - you can't scratch it, but someone else (who has the same out-of-reach itch) can. Therefore, you seek a fellow back-scratcher. When the two of you scratch each other's back (meet each other's needs), you both feel loved and cared for, and the relationship experiences a new and wonderful dimension - *intimacy*!

It's OK to have needs; it's not a sign of "weakness."

"Blessed are the poor in spirit (the needy), for theirs is the king-dom of heaven" (Matthew 5:4).

Unfortunately, in our society we have established a mentality that says, "If you're 'mature' (or in the case of the male ego, if you're 'tough'), then you won't have needs, or at least you won't admit to having them."

If you need comforting, there's something wrong with
   you.
If you need appreciation, you're insecure.
If you need support, you're weak.
If you need security, you lack faith.
If you need acceptance, you have a poor self image.

But to admit that we have needs is not an admission of *weakness*, it's a confession of our *humanity*. We all have needs...that's the way God made us...and to admit that we have needs is not only truthful, it's beneficial.

Unfortunately, this reluctance to admit that we have needs is often conveyed the most in **Christian circles**. We often succumb to a subtle but erroneous teaching that the more "mature" we become in Christ, the fewer needs we have and the less we need each other. Which, if taken to an extreme, produces a self-reliant, self-sufficient, egotistical, obnoxious, spiritual "Maverick."

The truth is, God has created us with needs so that we might constantly look to Him, allowing Him to minister to us through others, and so we will devote ourselves to unselfishly meeting other people's needs. This truth will produce a dependent, humble, unselfish, pleasant, spiritual "brother or sister," whose heart is full of gratitude for the fact that God, often through others, is meeting his/her needs and whose focus is on lovingly meeting the needs of family and friends.

Three dangers to avoid relative to needs

1. It's dangerous to *deny* our neediness.

"God opposes the proud but gives grace to the humble" (James 4:6).

One reason it's hazardous to deny needs is that if we deny our needs or if we think we can meet our own needs, we'll become pridefully self-reliant and self-sufficient. We'll rob ourselves of the joy of *receiving* from other people - and God.

Philippians 4:19 says, *"My God will meet all your needs according to His glorious riches."* First of all, if we don't have needs, this verse doesn't make much sense. But also, look at that word "meet," and the phrase "His riches." If we're self-sufficient, if we refuse to admit that we have needs, we'll never tap into God's supply - His riches. Those *"good and perfect gifts from above"* that the apostle James talked about (James 1:17) will never be ours if we don't "look up."

Incidentally, the Bible describes a church that suffered from this "I don't need anything" syndrome. The Lord said to the church at Laodicea, *"You say, 'I am rich; I have acquired wealth and **do not need a thing**.' But you do not realize that you are wretched, pitiful, poor, blind and naked"* (Revelation

3:17). Could this diagnosis be generally applied to anyone who says, "I don't need a thing"?

Another reason it's unhealthy to deny that we have needs is that if we're not willing to admit that we have needs, we'll be reluctant to acknowledge that other people have needs, and we'll be loathed to meet their needs. Here's how it works:

If I think I don't need *comfort* - I'll be slow to understand why my spouse needs comfort.

If I'm unwilling to admit that I need *attention* - I'll be disinclined to meet my children's need for attention.

If I think everyone ought to "bear their own burden," then I won't offer support to my friends when they're going through hard times.

When people attempt to share their needs with me, my attitude will be "What's wrong with you?" And I'll impatiently resort to criticism, lecturing, correcting, teaching, belittling, or just plain neglect.

When we begin to get in touch with our own neediness, we'll become more understanding, sympathetic, tolerant, patient, and loving.

2. It's dangerous to *exalt* our neediness.

"Do nothing out of selfish ambition or vain conceit, but in humility consider others better than yourselves" (Philippians 2:3).

Some people *deny* they have needs; others go to the opposite extreme and *exalt* their needs and become selfish and demanding. Unfortunately, when we become fixated on having our own needs met we often:

Miss out on the joy of giving - Jesus said, *"It is more blessed to give than to receive"* (Acts 20:35), so in this entire give/receive scenario, it's better to be on the giving end than the receiving end. But takers and demanders seldom give.

Miss out on the endless provision of God's blessing - Jesus said, *"Give and it will be given to you"* (Luke 6:38). Many people think that Jesus was just referring to money when He said this, but finances is not the topic in Luke 6. So what does the "it" refer to? "It" refers to whatever you need! "It" refers to whatever you have received from God...then give it to others, without fear of "running out." All that you have received from Him...His acceptance, forgiveness, comfort, and love...are kept in "circulation" by giving them away. It's one of those wonderful, divine, "makes-no-common-sense" principles that works every time. Your needs can't really be satisfied by *taking*, they must be lovingly and voluntarily *given to*. A miracle seems to take place as you "give away" that which you've graciously received...He gives back abundantly. But chances are, you won't do that if you're pre-occupied with exalting your own needs.

Become obnoxious - In describing the acts of the sinful nature, the apostle Paul placed the sin of selfishness among a disgusting group of vices, *"Hatred, discord, jealousy, fits of rage, **selfish ambition**, dissensions, factions"* (Galatians 5:20). Selfishness is a very distasteful characteristic. In other words, nobody wants to be around a selfish person. Focus exclusively on your own needs - and you'll become obnoxious. Your friends will be few.

3. It's dangerous to *condemn* our neediness.

"Therefore, there is now no condemnation for those who are in Christ Jesus" (Romans 8:1).

Self-condemnation is a subtle trap that says, "I know I have needs, but I feel guilty because I do"; or, "What's wrong with me? - I'm lonely." The truth is, if God created us with needs, then we're not selfish just because we're needy. In our fallen state, we may choose to behave selfishly as we try to "take" from others; but when we do, our sin is in the selfishness, not the neediness. Admitting we have needs is not a confession of wrong, it's an acknowledgment of our humanity and our "neediness" before God (Matthew 5:3).

Even Jesus, the God/man, had needs. Jesus, as portrayed in the Gospels, was not only a sinless Savior, but a person who expressed a need to relate intimately with His Father and with others.

Intimacy needs can only be met by emotional and spiritual *commodities*, administered through emotional and spiritual *beings*.

Your emotional and spiritual needs cannot be satisfied by **things**.

A car is not a substitute for *affection*.
A house cannot meet your need for *love*.
Degrees and diplomas will not satisfy your need for *respect*.
A position of authority is not an alternative for *comfort*.
Successful projects will not produce *peace*.

Emotional and spiritual needs can only be met by emotional and spiritual commodities:

Only *love* can satisfy your need for *love*.
Only *affection* will meet your need for *affection*.
Empathy is a source of *comfort*.
Forgiveness produces *peace*.

And emotional and spiritual commodities can only be met as part of *"God's grace in its various forms"* (1 Peter 4:10) as administered by emotional and spiritual beings: God, and other humans as God ministers through them.

The priority of needs is different for every individual.

While we all seem to have the same needs, the *priority* of those needs is different for each person. Your greatest need may be for *affection*, while your partner's greatest need may be *security*. One child may have an acute need for *comfort*, but another sibling's greatest need may be *encouragement*. *Appreciation* may be at the top of the list for your next door neighbor, while your tennis buddy needs *approval* more than anything else.

If we're not careful, we'll not only treat everyone the same (as if they all had the same priority of needs), but we'll go about meeting other people's needs based on what our priority of needs is. For instance, if your greatest need is for affection, you may gallantly and sincerely inundate your partner with affection without realizing that it may be at the bottom of his/her list. You might then become somewhat indignant if your partner isn't overwhelmed with gratefulness for your attentive "giving." It would be an innocent, well-meaning mistake, but a mistake nevertheless.

An important aspect of learning to love an individual is taking the time to know them and to discover what their unique needs are. Perhaps this is what Peter meant when he admonished husbands to, *"Live with your wives in an understanding way"* (1 Peter 3:7). It may also be a part of how a woman, *"Watches over the affairs of her household"* (Proverbs 31:27). With adults, it's not uncommon to discover that their most important individual needs are those which were either *not* met in childhood or those which *were* generously and sufficiently met. In other words, if I had no security growing up, I'll need a lot of it as an adult. On the other hand, if I had plenty of security growing up, I'll probably need a lot of it as adult simply because I was accustomed to receiving it and enjoyed feeling secure.

Needs - a key factor in love and intimacy.

There's a big difference between "surface" relationships and "intimate" relationships.

• It's possible to be around people all day long and still be lonely. Perhaps that's why a recent survey indicated that 70% of Americans say they are lonely.

• Some couples have been married for years, but there is no "oneness." Perhaps that's why the second highest rate of divorce is among those who have been married at least 25 years. The most common reason given for these divorces is "incompatibility." Can you imagine being married to someone for 25 years and then separating because you're mismatched? What does that say about the quality of the relationship during those 25 years?

Surface relationships are such that we can actually be around people constantly, but still be lonely. Tragically, it's possible to "hydro-plane" through life and never share the joys of intimacy with another human being. Unfortunately, that's exactly where most people live - in a world of superficial, unfulfilling relationships.

But God's plan for our lives involves us being "connected" to one another in a close and loving way. Instead of our relationships being distant, aloof, indifferent, formal, removed, limited, and superficial, they can be close, personal, deep, caring, affectionate, and warm. They can be *intimate*.

How is intimacy spawned? How is it deepened and maintained? When two people lovingly draw upon God's unlimited resources and meet one another's needs, the result is - intimacy. Needs, therefore, are the catalyst for intimacy, and intimacy is the by-product of needs being met.

In the next chapter we'll take a closer look at the top 10 intimacy needs.

Discussion Questions

1. Why did God create us with physical, soulish, and spiritual needs?
2. Do we ever grow out of these needs; can they be met once for all?
3. Did Jesus have needs? Did He ever express His needs to other people? If so, give some examples.
4. What are the likely outcomes if we deny that we have needs?
5. What are the likely outcomes if we exalt our needs?
6. What are the likely outcomes if we condemn ourselves concerning our needs?
7. How does the meeting of needs and the development of intimacy relate?
8. God created three divine relationships: marriage (Genesis 2), family (Genesis 4), and the church (Matthew 16). Realizing that we all have needs and that we cannot meet our own needs, what might be one reason why God created these three relationships?

Personal Assessment Questions

1. Do you think that you have emotional needs?
2. Do you tend to deny or exalt your needs? Or do you condemn yourself relative to your needs?
3. Do you acknowledge that those closest to you have needs and that you should be an agent for meeting their needs?
4. Do you ever get impatient at other people when they express their emotional needs?
5. Would it be helpful to memorize key Scriptures on this topic? Such as Philippians 4:19, Matthew 5:3, Philippians 2:3, Revelation 3:17, Romans 8:1.

Suggestions for Practical Application

1. Using Chart # 1 on pages 20-21, write down the names of your spouse, children, close relatives, and friends and then list what *you* think are their top 5 needs. Then ask the individuals what *they* think their top 5 needs are. Discuss the results.
2. Using Chart # 1, write down what your top 5 needs are. If you're married, ask your spouse to list what he/she thinks your top 5 needs are. Discuss the results.

Chart # 1 - Assessing The Unique Priority of Needs in Individuals

Although we all have the same basic needs, the *priority* of these needs may differ with each individual. A husband's greatest need may be respect, while his wife's greatest need may be attention. One child may particularly need affection, while another may be especially blessed by approval. If we're not careful, we'll not only treat everyone the same (as if they all had the same priority of needs), but we'll go about meeting other people's needs based on what our priority of needs are. An important aspect of learning to love an individual is taking the time to know them and to discover what their unique needs are.

Write down the names of your spouse, children, close relatives, and best friends and list (in order of priority) what *you* think their 5 most important needs are. Then ask them for *their* opinion. Consider these needs: acceptance, approval, encouragement, support, affection, security, respect, attention, comfort, appreciation.

Spouse (name)_____

    My opinion _____

    Their opinion _____

Child (name)_____

    My opinion _____

    Their opinion _____

Child (name)_____

    My opinion _____

    Their opinion _____

Child (name)_____

    My opinion _____

    Their opinion _____

Relative (name)_____
   My opinion _____
   Their opinion _____

Relative (name)_____
   My opinion _____
   Their opinion _____

Relative (name)_____
   My opinion _____
   Their opinion _____

Friend (name) _____
   My opinion _____
   Their opinion _____

Now write down *your* top 5 needs.

_____

Ask your spouse to write down what he/she thinks your top 5 needs are.

_____

Discuss the results during special times of sharing such as:
   • Marriage "staff" meetings - A designated time each week when husband and wife can vulnerably share issues of the heart.
   • Family nights - Special times of sharing which may include a family meal and fun activities.
   • Enrichment groups/classes - for couples, singles, or families.

Chapter 2 - The Top Ten Intimacy Needs

"Faithfully administering God's grace in its various forms"
(1 Peter 4:10).

God's grace "in its various forms" is like a multi-faceted diamond. The more "facets" or "sides" to the diamond, the more its value. In this chapter we'll identify and define the top 10 intimacy needs, offer some practical suggestions on how you can meet these needs in other people's lives, and show how meeting needs was an important part of Jesus's ministry and how God continually meets these needs in our lives.

We might begin by clarifying what constitutes a "valid" need. An intimacy need is a need that God has specifically met in your life. By meeting it, He has validated that it's all right to need it! For instance, the fact that God has accepted us means it's all right to need acceptance. The fact that He comforts us means comfort is a legitimate human need.

Attention

To take thought of another and convey appropriate care, interest, concern, and support; to enter into another's world.
"But that the members (of the body) should have the same care for one another"(1 Corinthians 12:25).

1. Spend time with people. There's no substitute for spending time with people. They're especially blessed when they realize that we're taking time out of our busy schedule to spend time with just *them*. Time is a valuable commodity; therefore it's a wonderful expression of attention.
2. Spend *individual* time with people. Don't just spend time with people in groups, but arrange for private time with individuals. Our need for attention is not met in groups. For instance, if you have three children, you need to spend private time with each child.

3. Go where people are - enter into *their* world. Have lunch with your child - at their school; if you have a business luncheon, pickup your client/friend at *his/her* office and ask for a tour. When your spouse/friend/child has a recital, concert, game, program, or awards ceremony - be there. This always requires the sacrifice of leaving *your* world - your agenda, priorities, and comfort zone.

4. Listen to people. Don't dominate conversations but encourage others to talk - and to talk about themselves - their feelings, goals, and plans. Try to talk where there won't be any interruptions and concentrate on the conversation; don't daydream or succumb to distractions.

Jesus met our ultimate need for attention by leaving His environment (heaven) and entering into our world; He became like us in order to personally relate to us and us to Him. During His earthly ministry, Jesus didn't spend time with just the masses but invested much of His time with individuals (Zaccheus, Nicodemus, the Samaritan woman, the disciples).

God continues to meet our need for attention by providing us with the privilege of prayer, whereby we may receive His individual, undivided, and unlimited attention. Furthermore, we are convinced of the individual attention He gives us, because the Bible says that He knows our thoughts (Psalm 139:2), counts the number of hairs on our head (Luke 12:7), knew us in our mother's womb (Psalm 139:13), and promises to provide for our every need (Matthew 6:25-34).

Acceptance

Deliberate and ready reception with a favorable response; to receive willingly; to regard as good and proper.

"Wherefore accept one another, just as Christ also accepted us to the glory of God" (Romans 15:7).

1. Look beyond people's faults and minister to their needs. The closer we get to someone, the more we notice their imperfections. Acceptance involves looking past these flaws and meeting their needs.

2. Quickly forgive others when personally offended. Unforgiveness short-circuits acceptance.

3. Help people to properly deal with their failures and disappointments. Our need for acceptance is accentuated when we experience a failure or when we are unduly disappointed. We need to notice when people experience a failure (real or perceived) or when they're disappointed (particularly in themselves) and minister to their need for acceptance. Acceptance is based upon a person's innate value to God as a person of special worth, and not on their performance or productivity.

4. Love people with God's unmerited, unconditional, and unlimited love. God's love for us is unmerited (we don't deserve it and can't earn it), unconditional (it's not based on what we do or don't do), and unlimited (it will never "run out" or be detained). We should accept and love others in like manner.

5. Be particularly sensitive to accept people who are in any way "different" from you. If people look different, talk differently, dress differently, have different customs, are of a different nationality, are of a different socio-economic background, or for any other reason are in the minority, they probably have an acute need to be accepted.

6. Be especially sensitive to people's need for acceptance when they enter into a new environment. When people move to a different city, school, church, or job, they have an acute need to be accepted into the new group.

Jesus met our ultimate need for acceptance in that *"while we were yet sinners"* He died for us (Romans 5:8); He looked beyond our faults and saw and met our needs. During His earthly ministry, Jesus accepted people where they were regardless of background, race, or condition (the Samaritan woman, the thief on the cross, the Gentile centurion, the woman caught in adultery); helped them deal with their failures (Peter's denial, disciples' lack of faith); loved people with unconditional love; and forgave freely ("Father forgive them...").

He continues to provide us with acceptance in that if we, *"Confess our sins, He is faithful and just and will forgive us our sins and purify us from all unrighteousness"* (1 John 1:9).

Appreciation

To recognize with gratitude; to communicate with words and feelings personal gratefulness for another person; to praise.

"I praise you..." (1 Corinthians 11:2).

1. Praise people verbally and publicly. When someone demonstrates a positive attitude or character trait or performs a positive deed - praise them. And verbal praise is particularly effective when stated *publicly*. To praise your spouse, friend, child, or employee is good, but to praise them *in front of other people* may even be better.

2. Focus on what people do that's right, not on what they do that's wrong. Some people have a "sin patrol" mentality - they try to catch people doing something wrong, bring it to their attention (and others'), and then administer punishment or rebuke. Instead, we should try to catch people doing something *right*, and then verbally and publicly praise them. Your spouse, children, employees, and friends will be more motivated by positive reinforcement than by negative comments.

3. Generously give cards, trophies, ribbons, plaques, and special gifts. Physical tokens of appreciation are very effective and usually long-lasting. The monetary value of a gift is relatively unimportant; it's the thought and effort that's important. "Special gifts" are particularly effective - become familiar with people's hobbies, what they collect, their favorite foods and drinks, and give them gifts which relate.

God met our ultimate need for appreciation as the Bible affirms us as saints (Romans 1:7), sons (Ephesians 1:5), joint-heirs (Romans 8:17), royal priests and people for God's own possession (1 Peter 2:9). During His earthly ministry, Jesus continually voiced appreciation to individuals: the Canaanite woman (Matthew 15:28), Mary of Bethany (Mark 14:6), a Centurion (Luke 7:9), John the Baptist (Luke 7:28), and a poor widow (Luke 21:3). God has promised to affirm and appreciate those who are faithful (2 Timothy 4:8, Luke 6:35, Ephesians 6:8).

Support/Bear Burden

To come alongside and gently carry a problem or struggle; to assist; to provide for.

"Carry each other's burdens, and in this way you will fulfill the law of Christ" (Galatians 6:2).

1. Anticipate and notice periods of "high stress" in other people's lives and be available to help. Times of high stress can be produced by: busy schedules, unemployment, illness, death in the family, divorce, financial instability, mid-life crisis, domestic problems, a move, or pressures at work. These stressful times can produce more pressure than one person can bear, in which case the support of others is necessary.

2. Offer to use personal resources to help support others. 1 John 3:17 says *"If anyone has material possessions and sees his brother in need but has no pity on him, how can the love of God be in him?"* Using personal resources can not only meet the practical need of those we're ministering to, but the individual will also be uniquely encouraged and blessed when they know that we are sharing out of our own resources.

3. Be willing to become personally involved and even to do "menial" tasks to help others. Burden bearing often requires that we do menial tasks which we normally don't have to do. We may need to: run errands, wash dishes,

baby-sit, do yard work, or house-sit. When this is necessary, the recipient of our support is uniquely touched by our willingness to do whatever it takes to help bear their burden.

God met our ultimate need for support by anticipating the great burden that we could not bear ourselves (the payment for our sins), and by committing His personal resources (His Son Jesus) to suffer earthly "menial" tasks (He suffered in all ways and was tempted in all ways). During His earthly ministry Jesus, invited the multitudes to *"Come to Me, all you who are weary and burdened, and I will give you rest"* (Matthew 11:28). When Jesus completed His earthly ministry, the Holy Spirit was given to believers as the Paraclete, the "One called alongside" who supports us as He teaches (John 16:12-15), comforts (Acts 9:31, John 14:16), assures (Romans 8:16), guides (Romans 8:14), and intercedes for us (Romans 8:26).

Encouragement

To urge forward and positively persuade toward a goal; to inspire with courage, spirit, or hope; to stimulate.
"Therefore encourage one another and build each other up" (1 Thessalonians 5:11).

1. Encourage others to set goals and then help them to achieve their goals. Encourage your spouse, children, and friends to live productive lives by helping them develop God-given plans and goals and then become actively involved in helping them reach those goals. If they're already goal-oriented, learn what their goals are and encourage them to succeed.
2. Recognize when others are discouraged and minister encouragement to them. Everyone goes through times of discouragement (we can even become "weary in well-doing"), and when we do, we need to be encouraged.

3. Encouragement can be administered through a phone call, card or letter, visit, or an appropriate word. Make it a habit to perform several encouraging gestures each day.

4. Let people know you're praying for them. If people perceive that you are a person of prayer, they'll be encouraged to know that you're praying for them. It's also very appropriate and effective to pray for people "right on the spot" instead of just saying, "I'll be praying for you."

5. When someone is discouraged, treat them to a special meal or a night out. When people are discouraged, just a change of routine is often encouraging. Treat them to dinner at their favorite restaurant, invite them over to see a movie, or spend a long weekend together.

God met our ultimate need for encouragement by providing us with an abundant life through Jesus (John 10:10), and by promising us that He will never leave us or forsake us (Hebrews 13:5). During His earthly ministry, Jesus continually encouraged His disciples and those who were downcast and discouraged. The Pharisees even criticized Him because He regularly met with those who were spiritually and emotionally sick (Matthew 9:12-13). God continually encourages us through the ministry of His word, the presence of His Spirit, and answered prayer.

Affection

To communicate care and closeness through physical touch and affirming words.
"Greet one another with a holy kiss" (Romans 16:16).

1. Using discretion, become more physical in your relationships. The appropriateness of certain gestures will be determined by the relationship:

Spouse - hold, caress, give body rub, hold hands, kiss. It's important that these physical gestures be performed, not as acts leading to sexual intimacy, but as expressions of emotional love and support.

Your own children - hold, kiss, hold hands, wrestle, hug.

Other children - hug, hold hands in an affirming manner, kiss on the forehead.

Friends - shake hands, hug, slap on the back, embrace.

2. Verbalize your love: speak words of love, kindness, and affection. It's particularly encouraging to speak spontaneous expressions which are "unmerited." For instance, you might say, "I've been thinking today about how special you are to me and how much I love you." If you have difficulty speaking words of love and affection, begin by sending cards and notes, then progress to verbal communication.

During His earthly ministry, Jesus was continually in physical contact with others. When Jesus healed, He often did so accompanied by physical contact (Matthew 8:3, 8:15, 9:29); He consoled His disciples accompanied by physical contact (Matthew 17:7); and He ministered to children through physical affection (Mark 10:16, Matthew 19:13).

Respect

To value and regard highly; to convey great worth; to esteem.

"Show proper respect to everyone" (1 Peter 2:17).

1. A general guideline of respect is that before making any commitment that impacts another person's life, take time to fully discuss it with them. For instance, marriage partners should discuss business commitments, trips, houseguests, major financial outlays, and other decisions *before* commitments are made. Parents should discuss with their children issues such as household chores and discipline measures.

2. Solicit, and show deference to, other people's opinions. Everyone is entitled to their opinion - regardless of gender

or age, and since opinions are so personal, the need for respect is satisfied when we ask people to share their opinions and particularly when we show deference to their opinions. For instance, instead of *telling* your family where they're going on vacation, *ask them* where they would like to go. Instead of handing down "orders" to your employees, allow them to be involved in the decision-making process.

3. Respect other people's property, privacy, and personal preferences. Take proper care of objects that you borrow and property you're on. If you borrow a friend's car, return it in better shape than you received it. When you're visiting someone's home or office, show proper respect for their property. Honor other people's right for privacy; knock before you enter your child's room; if your spouse wants to "be alone," honor his/her request. If your spouse wants the bathroom towels folded a certain way, honor his/her preference.

4. Respect other people's time. Always be prompt for appointments; being late indicates a disrespect for other people's schedules. In one sense, when we make others wait on us, we're robbing them of a valuable commodity - time.

5. Eliminate all prejudices, especially those regarding race, gender, and nationality, because none of these factors should inhibit our respect for another human being. Any form of cultural bias destroys respect.

During His earthly ministry, Jesus ignored all the social prejudices of His society by showing respect to tax collectors, Samaritans, the poor, lepers, and women. He treated all people as equals.

God considers us to be of such great worth that He sacrificed His only Son that we might be redeemed. Furthermore, He respects our individuality and the sovereignty of our wills by not forcing Himself or His will upon us but allowing each person to decide for himself whether or not he will receive what God has to offer.

Security

Freedom from exposure to danger; to put beyond hazard of losing, want, or deprivation; confidence of "harmony" in relationships.
"May those who love You be secure" (Psalm 122:6).

1. Provide "relational" security in all relationships. For instance, a husband should live in such a way that his wife knows he's a "one woman man" and that he will always be true to her. Friends should demonstrate a depth of commitment that will prevail through "thick and thin." Children should feel secure in knowing that their parents will always care for them and that divorce will never destroy the family unit.

2. Provide financial security for those to whom you're responsible. For instance, husbands and fathers should provide financial security for their families by: operating on a budget, adhering to scriptural principles of finances, having a good work ethic, developing marketable skills, producing adequate income, having a viable will, and providing a secure financial future. Employers can provide financial security for their employees by: adopting and adhering to fair employment policies, operating the business on scriptural principles, caring more for the well-being of people than for products, and providing adequate plans for employees' futures.

3. Let people know that you're aware of their physical, emotional, and spiritual needs and that you're committed to help meet those needs. We're "satisfied" when our needs are currently being met; we're "secure" when we know that our needs will be met in the future. For instance, relative to our need for food - we feel *satisfied* after consuming a delicious meal; we feel *secure* in knowing that we'll have food tomorrow and beyond. You can also minister security to others by verbally reassuring them of your love and attention, "I

just want you to know how committed I am to meeting your needs and loving you as God has loved me."

During His earthly ministry, Jesus offered security to those who were close to Him by continually meeting their physical, soulish, and spiritual needs. At times He even performed a miracle to meet a physical need such as the need for food (feeding of the five thousand).

God meets our need for security by promising never to leave us or forsake us (Joshua 1:5). He will always meet our need for food, clothing, and shelter (Matthew 6:25-32), and those who trust Jesus as Savior are eternally secure, *"I give them eternal life, and they shall never perish; no one can snatch them out of my hand"* (John 10:28).

Comfort

To give strength and hope to; to ease the grief or pain; to console, cheer.

"The God of all comfort, who comforts us in all our troubles, so that we can comfort those in any trouble..." (2 Corinthians 1:3,4).

1. Learn to recognize times when people have an increased need for comfort and be available and willing to minister to them. We have an acute need for comfort when: we've experienced rejection or disappointment; we're physically ill, under stress, or unemployed; we've lost a loved one in death; a tragedy has occurred; we've experienced the trauma of a divorce or separation; or when our "comfort zone" is challenged or violated (a job change, move to another city).

2. When someone needs comforting, refrain from correcting them ("The reason this happened is..."), teaching them ("Next time..."), giving them a "pep-talk" ("Come on, cheer up! It's a beautiful day outside!"), or giving advice ("If I were you, I'd..."). Instead, learn to *empathize* with those

who are hurting. Empathy involves identifying with the feelings of others - to hurt with those who hurt, to weep with those who weep. Comfort is an emotional need and cannot be met simply by intellectual instruction (such as correction, teaching, or giving advice).

3. Learn the "vocabulary of comfort" - phrases like, "I'm so sorry that you're hurting," "I hurt for you," "I love you, and I want to pray for you right now," "I'm on your side, and I'm committed to help you through this." These phrases can be communicated verbally or in writing.

4. In addition to verbal expressions of empathy, use appropriate gestures to administer comfort. If done discretely and sincerely, a warm embrace, holding hands, or wiping a fevered brow can bring comfort.

5. Perform specific deeds that will bring relief and comfort to the one hurting. You might: provide a hot meal, take care of children, or help with transportation needs.

Jesus ministered comfort throughout His earthly ministry, often identifying with the hurts of others to the degree that He wept with them (John 11:35, Luke 19:41). Even on the eve of His death, Jesus comforted His disciples (John 14:1,18; 16:33).

God is the *"God of all comfort"* (2 Corinthians 1:3), and the Holy Spirit is often referred to as the "Comforter" (John 14:16,26; 15:26; 16:7). The Greek word for comfort is "parakaleo" which means "to come to one's side, to one's aid" and suggests the ability to console and give aid.

Approval

To accept as satisfactory; to give formal or official sanction to; to have or express a favorable opinion; to approve of.

"Because anyone who serves Christ in this way is pleasing to God and approved by men" (Romans 14:18).

Approval is the proper response to righteous living. We must *accept* everyone, regardless of their actions (love the sinner, hate the sin), but *approval* involves commending and affirming a person because they have done what is right. Obviously, not everything nor everyone meets with God's approval (1 Corinthians 11:19). 2 Timothy 2:15 states that we should work/strive to be approved of God.

Approval is an important need because without it we may become "weary in well-doing." It is particularly important that those who are in authority commend their subordinates when they do what is right (1 Peter 2:14, Romans 13:3).

1. Notice when people: demonstrate admirable character traits, resist evil and stand for what is right, stand alone, persevere through difficult times, or take initiative to perform good deeds - and commend them verbally and publicly.

2. Carefully consider those who are under your authority; don't just correct them when they do wrong but communicate approval when they do well.

3. Approval can be expressed verbally or through physical gifts such as presents, a pay raise, or a bonus.

During His earthly ministry, Jesus continually expressed approval to those who did right - the widow, for giving all she had; Peter, for declaring that Jesus was the Son of God; Mary, for anointing Him with perfume; the Centurion, for his great faith; and a leper, for his gratitude. Even Jesus received approval from His Father when God said, *"This is My Son, whom I love; with Him I am well pleased"* (Matthew 3:17).

God meets our need for approval by "strengthening" us when our hearts are completely His (2 Chronicles 16:9), by answering our prayers when we are righteous (James 5:16) and pray according to His will (John 9:31), and by giving us peace (Philippians 4:9).

Discussion Questions

1. Relative to each of the top 10 needs, what are some of the possible outcomes if these needs are met in a person's life? What are possible outcomes if they are not met?
2. We've limited our discussion to the top 10 intimacy needs. List other emotional and spiritual needs that we all have.
3. Refer to Chart # 2 on page 38. Read the statements and write down what need is being expressed.

Personal Assessment Questions

1. When you were a child, were your top 10 intimacy needs met by your father? Were they met by your mother? Was there another significant person (grandparent, sibling, neighbor) who met these needs? Use Questionnaire # 1 on page 39 to record your answer.
2. If you're married, has your spouse met these needs in your life? Have you met your spouse's needs? Use Questionnaire # 2 on pages 40-41 to record your answers.
3. If you have children, have you met each child's needs? Use Questionnaire # 2 on pages 40-41 to record your answers.

Suggestions for Practical Application

1. Using Chart # 3 on pages 42-44, list some practical ways that you can meet the needs of your spouse, children, and friends.
2. Using the statements on page 38 as examples, list some phrases that you often hear your spouse, children, friends, and colleagues say which may be their unique way of expressing their needs.
3. Consider memorizing selected Scripture passages related to three of your key needs and three of your spouse's key needs.

4. Discuss the Personal Assessment Questions and Practical Applications during a marriage staff meeting, family night, or enrichment group/class.

Chart # 2 - Learning to identify people's needs by listening to what they say

Listed below are some phrases you might hear from your spouse, children, or friends. Beside each phrase, write down the need that's being expressed by each statement. Possible needs are:

Acceptance	Security
Approval	Respect
Encouragement	Attention
Support	Comfort
Affection	Appreciation

1. "You're too busy." _____
2. "Look what I did." _____
3. "Do you mind asking my opinion?" _____
4. "Will you always love me?" _____
5. "I just can't do this." _____
6. "I feel out of place." _____
7. "I've had a bad day." _____
8. "I feel like a failure." _____
9. "Could we spend more time together?" _____
10. "I'm really upset!" _____
11. "Hold me." _____
12. "Would you help me?" _____
13. "I have a big nose." _____
14. "What do you think of what I've done?" _____
15. "I can't do anything right!" _____
16. "I've had it!" _____
17. "You're always making all the decisions." _____
18. "I just want a place we can call home." _____

Questionnaire # 1 - Assessment of needs met or unmet by principle care-givers in childhood

When you were a child you had needs. Were these needs met by your principle care-givers? On a scale from 1-10 (1 = needs were totally neglected, 10 = needs were lovingly and adequately met) write down how your needs were met by your mother, father, and any other care-givers (grandparents, siblings, neighbors). If some of your numbers are "low," be careful not to minimize this. Be truthful about your perceptions and feelings. No one is being portrayed as "bad" and no one will be "blamed." Often, someone can have a caring heart toward us but not meet our important needs

Need	Mother	Father	_____(other)
Acceptance	_____	_____	_____
Approval	_____	_____	_____
Encourage- ment	_____	_____	_____
Support	_____	_____	_____
Affection	_____	_____	_____
Security	_____	_____	_____
Respect	_____	_____	_____
Attention	_____	_____	_____
Comfort	_____	_____	_____
Appreciation	_____	_____	_____

Questionnaire # 2 - Assessment of how needs are being met in the family relationship

One of the joys and responsibilities of marriage is meeting your partner's needs. On a scale from 1-10 (1 = needs are totally neglected, 10 = needs are lovingly and adequately met) write down how each need is being met in your life by your spouse and then write down how you think you rate relative to meeting your spouse's needs.

Need	Rate how your spouse is meeting these needs in your life.	Rate how you think you are meeting these needs in your spouse's life.
Attention	_____	_____
Approval	_____	_____
Encouragement	_____	_____
Support	_____	_____
Affection	_____	_____
Security	_____	_____
Respect	_____	_____
Attention	_____	_____
Comfort	_____	_____
Appreciation	_____	_____

One of the special challenges of parenthood is to be available to give to your children's needs. Rate yourself on how well you think have met your children's needs. For older children, you might give them the opportunity to complete Questionnaire # 1 , asking them to give their perception of whether or not their needs are currently being met.

Need	Rate how you think you are meeting these needs in your child's (children's) life (lives).
Attention	_____
Approval	_____
Encourage-ment	_____
Support	_____
Affection	_____
Security	_____
Respect	_____
Attention	_____
Comfort	_____
Appreciation	_____

Chart # 3 - Practical ways to meet other people's needs

List some practical ways that you can meet the needs of your spouse and children.

Spouse:

Acceptance _____

_____

Approval _____

_____

Encouragement _____

_____

Support _____

_____

Affection _____

_____

Security _____

_____

Respect _____

_____

Attention _____

_____

Comfort _____

_____

Appreciation _____

Children:

Acceptance _____

_____

Approval _____

_____

Encouragement _____

_____

Support _____

_____

Affection _____

_____

Security _____

_____

Respect _____

_____

Attention _____

_____

Comfort _____

_____

Appreciation _____

_____

Friends:

Acceptance _____

_____

Approval _____

_____

Encouragement _____

_____

Support _____

_____

Affection _____

_____

Security _____

_____

Respect _____

_____

Attention _____

_____

Comfort _____

_____

Appreciation _____

_____

Chapter 3 - Needs (Met and Unmet) Affect Our Thinking, Feeling, and Behavior

To understand the impact that needs have on our lives, let's consider the **needs formula**.

A simple version of the formula is:

When needs are met, we feel good.
When needs are neglected, we feel bad.

An expanded version is:

Needs met = satisfaction, contentment, feelings of being loved and cared for.
Needs unmet = frustration, anxiety, dissatisfaction.

To illustrate the validity of this formula, consider some of your physical needs. You have a need for sleep, and after a good night's sleep you feel satisfied and contented. But if you go for several days without sleep, you begin to feel edgy, irritable, and frustrated. The same applies to your need for food. Following a good meal you feel gratified and fulfilled, but if you go for an extended period of time without eating, you feel discontented, touchy, and frustrated.

If this formula applies to physical needs, do you think it would also apply to emotional and spiritual needs? The answer to that is a resounding **yes**! If our needs for attention, approval, and appreciation are neglected, the result is not good. If these needs are met, the outcome is positive.

As a matter of fact, as our needs are met or unmet, we tend to unknowingly progress through a process which involves how we think, how we feel, and eventually how we behave.

The process goes like this:

Needs met = Healthy Thinking → Positive Emotions → Productive Behavior

Needs unmet = Unhealthy Thinking → Damaged Emotions → Negative Behavior

Our God-given needs are so strong and persistent, they will eventually affect our behavior.

The diagram on page 47 illustrates, in more detail, the progression from needs to behavior.

Let's look at two case studies and see how these two formulas work.

Sally and Bob have been married for fifteen years. In the early years of their marriage, mutual affection, attention, and encouragement freely flowed through open lines of communication. There was a touch of romance in their relationship.

But with each passing year the **quantity** of communication became less, consisting of nothing more than short quips like, "Uh-huh. OK. We'll talk about it later. I'm too tired."; and the **quality** of communication digressed from intimate, vulnerable topics to mundane and practical topics.

Eventually, Bob's daily routine consisted of: work, dinner, newspaper, T.V., and sleep. And the routine minimized his contact with Sally.

Sally's quest for attention, affection, and security began with pleas, quickly escalated to demands, and when that didn't work, she nagged and yelled; but eventually she just gave up. Bob refused to meet her needs.

The unfulfilling relationship took an emotional toll on Sally and she became depressed. Her doctor prescribed medication and suggested that she take a part-time job, just to get out of the house.

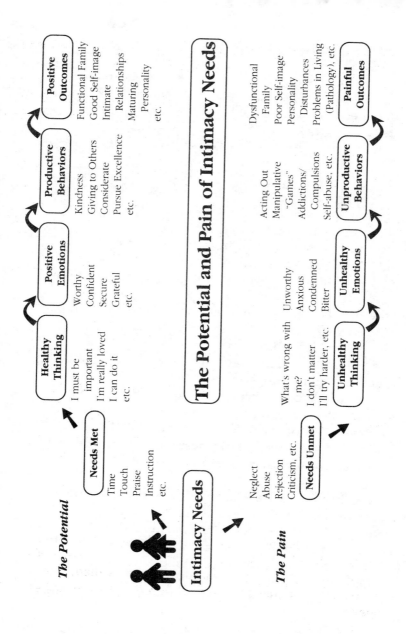

The Potential and Pain of Intimacy Needs

The Potential

Intimacy Needs

Needs Met
Time
Touch
Praise
Instruction
etc.

Healthy Thinking
I must be important
I'm really loved
I can do it
etc.

Positive Emotions
Worthy
Confident
Secure
Grateful
etc.

Productive Behaviors
Kindness
Giving to Others
Considerate
Pursue Excellence
etc.

Positive Outcomes
Functional Family
Good Self-image
Intimate Relationships
Maturing Personality
etc.

The Pain

Needs Unmet
Neglect
Abuse
Rejection
Criticism, etc.

Unhealthy Thinking
What's wrong with me?
I don't matter
I'll try harder, etc.

Unhealthy Emotions
Unworthy
Anxious
Condemned
Bitter

Unproductive Behaviors
Acting Out
Manipulative "Games"
Addictions/Compulsions
Self-abuse, etc.

Painful Outcomes
Dysfunctional Family
Poor Self-image
Personality Disturbances
Problems in Living (Pathology), etc.

This chart is from *Intimate Encounters*, 1994. Thomas Nelson Publishers. Used by permission.

Sally took a job working in a large insurance agency. She enjoyed her work because it made her feel needed and it gave her a renewed sense of identity. She worked in the same office as Larry - a kind, gentle divorcee. He was always complimenting Sally for her appearance and work.

One day, while they were taking a coffee-break together, Larry asked, "Sally, you look a little sad today, is something troubling you?" For the first time in years, she felt like someone genuinely cared for her. So she shared, from the depths of her heart, her loneliness, frustration, and despair.

During future coffee-breaks, their conversations became more and more transparent. Larry shared the details surrounding his divorce and Sally empathized with him. Through the months, a seemingly innocent friendship became an emotional affair. Legitimate emotional and intimacy needs were being met, but in a wrong way.

Multiple coffee-breaks led to lunch dates which led to after-work conversations. One night, when Bob was out of town, Sally went to Larry's apartment to see his new stereo system. As the evening progressed, the unthinkable happened.

As Sally's needs were not met at home, she slowly digressed through this process:

Needs Unmet - "I need attention, approval, respect, affection, and encouragement from my husband but I'm not getting it. He won't even spend time with me."

Unhealthy Thinking - "What's wrong with me? I must be unimportant. I don't matter. I'll try harder. Nothing will ever change."

Damaged Emotions - "I feel hurt, bitter, anxious, insecure, and lonely."

Unproductive Behavior - Denial, acting-out, manipulative games, seeking for needs to be met in illegitimate ways.

Painful Outcomes - Depression, outbursts of anger, "shutting down" of emotions, infidelity.

Both Sally's wrong responses and her pain were important to God. Her loneliness never "justifies" her wrong responses, but God cares about both her sinfulness and her loneliness.

To illustrate how the process can progress from met needs to positive outcomes, let's consider another case study.

Dave has a ten-year-old son named Jeffrey. Although Dave is a busy executive, every week he makes it a priority to spend time with his son. And instead of spending time doing "man" things, they do "kids" stuff. Dave often takes Jeffrey to the video arcade shop, looking for baseball cards, or to eat at - where else? - McDonalds.

Every kid has a need for attention, and Jeffrey's need is regularly met by his loving and caring father.

As Jeffrey's need for attention is lovingly and consistently met, he will tend to progress through this process.

Needs Met - "Dad's taking time out of his busy schedule just to spend time with me. He often stops doing something he likes to do in order to give me attention and approval."

Healthy Thinking - "I must be important, I'm really loved. I can do it! My father loves and cares for me."

Positive Emotions - "I feel secure, confident, worthy, and grateful."

Positive Behaviors - Kindness, giving to others, demonstration of godly character, gratitude, meeting other people's needs.

Positive Outcomes - Obedience, loyalty, productive work, good self-image, ability to develop intimate relationships, maturing personality.

We're motivated by needs

Another important factor to understand is: **We are moti-vated by needs**; that is, we're motivated to get our needs met, even if it means having them met in illegitimate ways. Our "fallen-ness" or sinfulness tends to exert powerful influence on us as we seek to have our needs met in invalid, illegitimate ways:

Searching for love, a teenager will sacrifice moral purity.
Motivated by a need for respect, a businessman will become a workaholic.
Needing attention but not getting it, a child will scream and cry.
In a quest for affection, a marriage partner will have an affair.
Hoping to find forgiveness, a person may become "works" oriented.

That's exactly what happened to Sally in the case study mentioned above. Her legitimate needs were not being met by her husband, so rather than find God's source of provision, she gradually drifted towards someone who *would* meet her needs. Our needs exert such a strong pull, we tend to gravitate towards those who will meet our needs, even if it compromises our convictions or morals.

This explains why people join gangs even though most gangs are socially reprehensible. Gangs are often composed of people who have been rejected by their principle caregivers. They often didn't have their needs met in a legitimate social environment (family, church), so they joined a social group that will accept them for who they are. As a member of the gang, they have a sense of identity and feel accepted, approved of, secure, and even appreciated.

People tend to go where their needs are being met.

This truth should have tremendous implications for the church. Charles Swindoll says, "Churches need to be less like national shrines and more like local bars...less like un-touchable cathedrals and more like well-used hospitals, places to bleed rather than monuments to look at...places where you can take your mask off and let your hair down...places where you can have your wounds dressed."

When churches begin to meet people's deep-felt needs, our buildings won't be able to contain the crowds. If we don't meet their needs, they'll continue to go to local bars, the bowling alley, the race track, and social clubs to have their needs met, or, they'll give up on having their needs met and give in to the "cocooning" of society, isolating them-selves in their homes, looking to the T.V. or computer as their only link to the outside world.

Unfortunately, we often concentrate on people's unpro-ductive *behavior* instead of their *unmet needs*. We then try to *correct* their behavior instead of *meeting* their needs. Hospi-tals, detention centers, and prisons are full of needy people.

We recently met with a 4th-grade boy who was having some behavioral problems at school. He was a good kid who had never been in trouble before, but he suddenly started talking in class and passing notes. His punishment was having to stay after school - just he and his teacher.

His mother brought him in for counseling, and after visiting with him about "kid's stuff" (so as to put him at ease), we asked this question, "When do you feel most loved and cared for?" His immediate response was, "When my teacher spends time with just me, after school, and she's not getting paid for it."

We soon discovered that his mother was working a 3:00 to 11:00 shift so she wasn't able to spend a lot of time with her son. The boy had a very acute need for attention which was being neglected, so he decided to do something about it. He discovered that he could act up in school and get some personal attention from someone whom he loved and re-spected - his teacher.

One approach to having solved this problem would be to focus on, and attempt to change, the boy's behavior - sepa-rate him from his classmates, take his pencils away, punish him more severely, or give him a lecture about the woes of misbehavior and rebellion. He probably would have become worse. An alternate approach would simply be for his parents to spend more time with him and give him the attention he so desperately needed. Which strategy do you think would work best?

Listed below are the top 10 intimacy needs we've identified and some possible outcomes if these needs are met or not met. You'll notice that often the likely outcomes are extremely different. For instance, when people's need for attention is not met, some may become boisterous and extroverted (demanding attention), while others may become reclusive and introverted (having giving up on having their needs met, they choose to "close up," instead of facing more pain).

Attention - Met - good self-image, confident, feelings of "I'm important," secure, willing to be a servant; attentive to other's needs.
Unmet - promiscuous, boisterous, poor self-image, feelings of being worthless, delinquency, shy and withdrawn, concentration on appearance.

Acceptance - Met - secure, confident, feelings of worth, relaxed, peaceful.
Unmet - performance oriented, workaholic, poor self-image, insecure; defensive.

Appreciation - Met - positive and optimistic, good work ethic, grateful, encouraging to others.
Unmet - easily discouraged and pessimistic, performance oriented, insecure, self-doubt.

Support - Met - encouraged, grateful, feelings of being loved, hope, sensitive to "giving" opportunities.
Unmet - discouraged, weariness toward life, fear of failure, timidity.

Encouragement - Met - "Can do" attitude, positive and optimistic, creative, productive.
Unmet - lack of confidence, failure complex, defeatist attitude, pessimistic, frustrated, withdrawn, negative.

Affection - Met - secure, free to give, feelings of being loved and comforted.
Unmet - aloof and distant, uncomfortable being physically close to people, cold and unfeeling, promiscuous, flirting, clinging to others of the opposite sex, unclear behaviors with opposite sex.

Approval - Met - productive, confident, good self-image.
Unmet - search for approval, performance oriented, workaholic, "self-made," lack of self-confidence, insecure, confused, fearful.

Security - Met - full of faith, confident, giving, grateful, positive, adaptable, flexible.
Unmet - fearful, insecure, controlling, possessive, anxious, worrier, negative, rigid, self-reliant.

Comfort - Met - caring, compassionate, positive, giving, sensitive, self-confident, loving.
Unmet - unable to comfort others, feelings of being alone and empty, volatile, promiscuous, avoidance of emotions, emphasis on "fixing" situations and people, obsessive-compulsive orientation.

Respect - Met - respectful of others, freedom to "grow up," giving, sensitive, high self-worth, loving, positively assertive.
Unmet - feelings of worthlessness and inferiority, insecure, demanding, intolerant, "victim" mind-set.

Needs (met or unmet) *do* affect our thinking, emotions, and ultimately our behavior.

Discussion Questions

1. Often, we focus solely on people's bad behavior and then attempt to simply "correct" their behavior. Realizing that bad behavior is usually a symptom of neglected needs being handled in an inappropriate manner, what would be a more productive approach to dealing with behavioral problems?
2. Do you think there's any correlation between our needs being abundantly met and the "abundant life" that Jesus promised in John 10:10?
3. Realizing the tremendous "pull" that needs have, why are people attracted to bars, clubs, and social organizations such as Kiwanis, Lion's Club, and Shriners? What implications does this have for ministry? Church outreach?

Personal Assessment Questions

1. Refer back to Questionnaire # 1 on page 39 and consider again to what degree some of your key needs were met as a child. Realizing that needs (met and unmet) affect our thinking, feeling, and behavior, how might you have been affected by your childhood experiences? Review some of your "low" scores from page 39 and the "symptoms" from pages 52-53 , perhaps circling some of the "symptoms" you see in your life. What aspect of your present behavior can be traced back to met and unmet needs?
2. Complete Chart # 4 on pages 56-57 which will help you establish a correlation between people's unproductive behavior and possible neglected needs.
3. Study Christ's ministry to Zacchaeus in Luke 19 to identify his "bad" behavior, his possible unmet needs, how Christ met his needs, and how Zacchaeus' behavior changed.

Suggestions for Practical Application

1. Become more sensitive to people's verbal and non-verbal communication. Resist "reacting" to their bad behavior and try to see beyond what they say and do to recognize their needs.

2. Review other biblical examples of Christ "looking beyond a person's faults and ministering to their needs."

3. When our needs have been met or are currently being met, the natural response is - gratitude. It's this gratitude that deepens our gratefulness toward others and our thanksgiving and worship toward God. Using Chart # 5 on pages 58-59, consider those who have done a good job meeting your needs and then make plans to express gratitude to them. This could be done through verbal expressions or through gifts, cards, and letters.

4. Consider discussing the Personal Assessment Questions and Suggestions for Practical Application during marriage staff meetings, family nights, or enrichment groups/classes.

Chart # 4 - Identifying the relationship between unproductive behavior and unmet needs

In most cases, unproductive behavior is the result of unmet needs being handled in an inappropriate way. An infant may cry, seeking affection; a child may color on the wall, seeking attention; a teenager may pursue unwholesome relationships, seeking approval; a businessman may become a workaholic, seeking respect.

In our attempt to correct the situation, we often focus only on the aberrant behavior, ignoring a critical underlying issue - unmet needs. A more productive approach would be to see the correlation between behavior and unmet needs and begin meeting the needs.

Write down the names of those closest to you (spouse, children, friends), list some of their alleged behavior problems, and then try to establish a link to unmet needs.

Name _____

Unproductive conduct _____

_____

Neglected needs possibly related to this conduct _____

_____

Name _____

Unproductive conduct _____

_____

Neglected needs possibly related to this conduct _____

_____

Name _____

Unproductive conduct _____

_____

Neglected needs possibly related to this conduct _____

_____

Name _____

Unproductive conduct _____

_____

Neglected needs possibly related to this conduct _____

_____

Name _____

Unproductive conduct _____

_____

Neglected needs possibly related to this conduct _____

_____

Name _____

Unproductive conduct _____

_____

Neglected needs possibly related to this conduct _____

_____

Chart # 5 - Establishing a journal of gratefulness

"Forget not all His benefits" (Psalm 103:2).

Gratefulness is the appropriate response to having our needs met. It's important to have an "attitude of gratitude." Record the names of those who have met your needs in the past and those who are currently being used of God to meet your ongoing needs. Thank God for their input in your life and then plan on expressing gratitude to these individuals. This could be done by a phone call, a letter, or a gift.

Individual who has given to meet my needs _____
How I'm going to express my appreciation to them:

_____

_____

Individual who has given to meet my needs _____
How I'm going to express my appreciation to them:

_____

_____

Individual who has given to meet my needs _____
How I'm going to express my appreciation to them:

_____

_____

Individual who has given to meet my needs _____
How I'm going to express my appreciation to them:

_____

_____

Individual who has given to meet my needs _____
How I'm going to express my appreciation to them: _____

_____

_____

Individual who has given to meet my needs _____
How I'm going to express my appreciation to them: _____

_____

_____

Individual who has given to meet my needs _____
How I'm going to express my appreciation to them: _____

_____

Assignment: Write a short prayer of gratefulness and
thanksgiving as you reflect on God's gracious provision to
you through other people.

_____

_____

_____

_____

Chapter 4 - Dealing With Unmet Needs

In the last chapter we discussed the potential positive and negative outcomes of having our needs met or neglected. Since "meaningful others" in our lives play a powerful and possibly painful role in our needs being met, what if some of these meaningful others have been neglectful or actively abusive? What can we do if our parents blew it in some ways? And what can we do if our needs are not currently being met? What can we do if we've hurt others by not meeting their needs? If there are no solutions to these dilemmas, we'll not only be bound to suffer the consequences for the rest of our lives but we'll have a miserable existence. God's promise of John 10:10 would be forfeited and despair would be our only recourse. The good news is: Our loving God *has* provided a way of healing, restoration, and contentment.

What to do if your needs have been neglected in the past

How do you deal with the fact that you've been hurt in the past by your parents, siblings, or friends? Often, needs are not only neglected but they're actively abused. For instance, a child's need for attention and acceptance can not only be neglected but it can be abused through verbal, physical, or sexual misuse. How can you gain freedom from the hurt and pain of past neglect and abuse? We suggest three steps:

1. Identify and acknowledge your hurts.
"In this world you will have trouble" (John 16:33).

Hurts cannot be healed if they are ignored. Emotional "baggage" caused by unmet needs doesn't just "go away" with time. Feelings of anger, bitterness, fear, shame, and guilt must be properly dealt with. The first step is to acknowledge the sadness, pain, hurt, and loss you felt when your needs were neglected. Then acknowledge any feelings of anger, bitterness, or resentment that might have developed as a result of the initial neglect and hurt. It often helps to talk about these feelings with a spouse or close friend - a "journey-mate."

2. Forgive your offenders.
"Get rid of all bitterness, rage and anger" (Ephesians 4:31).

Forgiveness is a choice, not primarily a feeling. The question is not "do you *feel* like forgiving, but *will* you?" Forgiveness is a conscious decision on our part to relieve the debt of our offender and let go of our anger and bitterness. Forgiveness is primarily for our benefit; it brings healing to our lives, regardless of any change or lack of change in the offender. We should forgive:

- whether or not our offender asks our forgiveness,
- even if our offender's behavior hasn't changed,
- even if we don't "feel like" forgiving.

Forgiveness is primarily a matter of stewardship. We forgive because we have been forgiven (Colossians 3:13, Ephesians 4:32, Matthew 18). It's often helpful to thoroughly explore how I've hurt others (See page 73) and experience the *sorrow* of my guilt and the gratefulness of God's forgiveness. This gratitude for my being forgiven empowers me to forgive others. It's also important that I verbalize my choice to forgive to God and to my spouse/friend.

3. Mourn your hurt.
Matthew 5:4 presents an important truth which will help produce emotional wellness, *"Blessed are those who mourn, for they will be comforted."*

Many people think of mourning as something to be done only when someone close to us dies. But we also need to mourn any and all losses that we as individuals suffer in day-to-day living. In other words, it's OK, and even necessary, to mourn *personal* losses.

Many times we're not inclined to mourn because we're not convinced that there will be someone there to love and comfort us. To mourn without being comforted just adds to the pain. This is yet another reason why we need loving, trusting relationships in which we can vulnerably share our hurts. We can't comfort ourselves - God wants to involve a spouse or friend in providing the empathy we need.

It takes emotions to heal emotions. That's why comfort is the prescribed solution for hurt and pain; not instruction, advice, pep-talks, or lectures. But we often offer these substitutes when the real need is for comfort. Here's how the various responses might sound:

Person needing comfort - "I lost my job last week. I was fired with no explanation."
Various responses:

Instruction - "Take a few days off, look at the classified ads, get your resume ready."
Advice - "If I were you, I'd get a lawyer to write a letter to your former employer."
Lecture - "The reason you got fired is..."
Pep-talk - "Cheer up. Everything will be OK. I'm sure you'll get a better job."
Comfort - "I'm sorry you lost your job. I hurt for you. You probably feel a great degree of hurt and loss. I want to pray for you. I promise to stand by you during this difficult time."

To establish and maintain emotional wellness, we must not only learn to mourn our own hurts but we must become adept at ministering comfort to those who hurt.

What to do if your needs are currently not being met

If your needs are currently not being met, we have three suggestions:

1. Communicate your needs. *"Speak the truth in love"* (Ephesians 4:15). When our needs are not being met by "meaningful others" (our spouse, parents, close friend, etc.), we must learn to vulnerably and lovingly communicate what we need without focusing on their negative behavior.

This vulnerability in sharing need allows us to exhibit and live out our faith...faith that God wants to provide, faith that He can work through others and faith that if we're rejected or let down by others - He remains faithful to us.

For instance, let's say your need for *attention* is being neglected. You know what the problem is - your spouse is working too much; and too many hours at the office means too few hours with you. Your initial reaction might be to focus on your partner's negative behavior (working too much, neglecting you) in which case you might say something like this:

"You're working too much. All you care about is your job. You love it more than you do me. You've always been selfish, and it's just getting worse!" (This would be sharing "truth" - but not in love.)

Or, you could lovingly communicate what you need, which might sound like this:

"Sweetheart, I love you, and miss spending time with you. I appreciate the fact that you work hard, but at the same time, I need you. Could we plan some time together, just for us?"

Which approach do you think would solicit the most favorable response?

Here's another example. Perhaps at your office your need for *respect* is being slighted. Decisions are being made that affect your life and career but no one is asking your opinion.

One way to respond would be to sulk, become moody, and begin the "silent treatment." (This would be violating Ephesians 4:15 by not speaking the truth.) You might also decide that whatever decision is made, you're going to dig your heels in the ground and resist forward progress. *That's* how you're going to let them know that they should have consulted you.

An alternate approach would be to communicate your hurt and suggest a different method of decision making. That might sound like this:

"I enjoy working for this company and want to do all that I can to help it be successful. I would appreciate being able to share, along with everyone else, my ideas about how we can accomplish certain tasks. Also, I would appreciate having input into decisions that will directly affect my life and work."

It's important to learn how to vulnerably and lovingly share your needs.

2. Look to God. God's sovereign design is that many of our needs be met through marriage, family, and the church. This is His way of making us inter-dependent with one another and in the midst of meeting each other's needs, love and intimacy are spawned - we experience part of the "oneness" Christ prayed for in John 17.

Our expectancy and faith must always be directed toward God, realizing that He may involve others in His ministry to us. But *He* is always available. When meaningful others fail us or are unavailable, He remains faithful. During our daily devotional time with Him, it is critical to receive His nurturing and provision.

David, the king of Israel, often received what he needed directly from the hand of the Lord. In 1 Samuel 30:6 we read that, *"David was greatly distressed because the men were talking of stoning him; each one was bitter in spirit because of his sons and daughters."* At this particular time in his life, David didn't have his friend Jonathan or his wife to talk to; he was alone. So what did David do? *"David found strength in the Lord his God."*

Hours before His death, when Jesus was in agony in the garden of Gethsemane, He looked to His disciples for comfort and encouragement. *"My soul is overwhelmed with sorrow to the point of death. Stay here and keep watch with me"* (Matthew 26:38); but they neglected Him, *"Then He returned to His disciples and found them sleeping"* (verse 40). But God the Father did not leave Him without help for, *"An angel from heaven appeared to Him and strengthened Him "* (Luke 22:43).

God knows our needs, and He is committed to seeing that they are met. When the "secondary" source of His supply is not functioning properly, He will directly meet our needs.

3. **Give to others.** As we mentioned in Chapter 1, Luke 6:38 presents a simple but profound truth, *"Give and it will be given to you."* What does the "it" refer to? Many people think that "it" refers to money, but in the preceding verses, money is never specifically mentioned. Actually, Jesus is discussing several different issues: love, judgment, and forgiveness.

The "it" in this verse refers to whatever you "give." If you give forgiveness, you'll get forgiveness. If you judge others, you'll be judged yourself. If you give love, you'll receive love. This verse teaches the same truth stated in Galatians 6:7, *"A man reaps what he sows."*

Now let's apply this verse to your unmet needs. Is your need for comfort being neglected? Then call upon God as the God of all comfort who will comfort you and then give you a way to comfort others. Is no one encouraging you? Instead of sulking about it, begin to encourage others. Whatever it is that you need - *receive* from God and then *give* it to others!

By giving to others, you'll not only be able to experience the promise of Luke 6:38, but you'll enjoy the blessing of Acts 20:35, *"It is more blessed to give than to receive."*

So if your needs aren't currently being met: learn to vulnerably share your needs, look to God as the ultimate source of supply, and give to others what you yourself need.

What to do if you have neglected or abused other people's needs

Because we are all sinful people living in a fallen world, hurtful experiences in all relationships are inevitable. Regardless of whether you've been married 6 months or 20 years, you have hurt your spouse. Regardless of whether your children are 2 years old or 20 years old, you have neglected and offended them. Hurt is inevitable; the question is, are you going to take the proper steps to heal these hurts. Here's what we suggest.

1. Identify how you have neglected or abused others and attempt to understand the gravity of your wrong.

How *have* you hurt your spouse? How *have* you hurt your children? Your friends? At this point don't let your mind wander to how they have hurt you; only consider how you've hurt them. (Matthew 7 challenges each of us to first deal with the "log" in our own eye before we try to deal with the "speck" in our friend's eye.)

Then, try to understand the depth to which you have hurt them and even try to enter into their sorrow. There's nothing more disgusting than a half-hearted, flippant confession. 2 Corinthians 7:10 speaks of a sorrow that leads to repentance. Are you sorrowful about your actions? Do you feel remorse? Regret? When you truly allow God to impact you with the severity of your sin, a godly sorrow comes that will produce a change in your behavior.

2. Confess your sin to God and to the individual.

"If we confess our sins, He is faithful and just and will forgive us our sins" (1 John 1:9).

"Therefore confess your sins to each other" (James 5:16).

Your neglect has offended at least two people, God and the individual, so you must confess to both. As used in the Bible, to "confess" means "to speak the same thing," so confession involves saying the same thing about our behavior as God says. God says sin is **wrong**. God says our sin is why His Son had to die. It's often helpful to meditate on Isaiah 53 and personalize the phrases, (*He was pierced for* **my** *transgressions*.) As we realize our own part in why Christ had to die, God will bring a brokenness and a contriteness of heart which will produce repentance. Next, receive the promise of God's forgiveness (1 John 1:9) and be grateful. Confession is genuine when it produces godly sorrow and subsequent gratefulness. Here are some characteristics of a proper confession.

- **Be specific in naming your sin.**

    Which of these two statements is more effective?

    "If I've offended you or hurt you in any way, I'm sorry."
    "I've been very selfish and insensitive. That's wrong of me."

    It's not only helpful to identify the sin, but to give examples. You might say, "I've been selfish and insensitive by working too much and not spending time with you. At times, I've even chosen church activities over you. That's wrong of me."

- **Use the words "I'm wrong" instead of "I'm sorry."**

    To simply say "I'm sorry" might only mean, "I'm sorry I got caught" or, "I'm sorry you're so sensitive" or, "I'm sorry we can't get along." Whereas to say, "I was wrong" is a true admission of guilt.

- **Don't offer excuses.**

    Our natural tendency is to confess that we were wrong, then offer excuses ("The reason I did that was..."), or we try to spread out the blame ("I was wrong, but I wouldn't have done it if you hadn't..."). Put a period after your confession - "I was wrong."

- **Ask, "Will you forgive me?"**

    At this point, the ball is in their court. Forgiveness is an act of the will; it is a choice, not primarily a feeling. If they forgive you, all of the negative aspects of a damaged relationship can be healed.

    But what happens if they don't forgive you? If you have sincerely apologized, that's all you can do. God will relieve you of any guilt associated with the relationship and you will be free. It would even be appropriate to communicate "I'll look forward to when you might choose to forgive me." Then it's clear who should make the next move. The individual who refuses to forgive will be tormented by their unforgiveness (Matthew 18:34).

Discussion Questions

1. Have you ever sensed that God was directly meeting your needs? Take time to reflect on specific examples and what needs in your life God was meeting.
2. Ephesians 4:15 says, *"Speak the truth in love."* How would this Scripture relate to the importance of our sharing with others the specific needs we have?
3. Read Matthew 18:21-35. What does this passage teach about forgiveness?

Personal Assessment Questions

1. Are your intimacy needs in relationships currently being met? If not, have you shared this with "meaningful others" in your life?
2. When was the last time you spoke these words, "I was wrong. Will you forgive me?" Given the fact that we are all sinful humans living in a fallen world, these phrases should probably be quite common. What hinders you from this vulnerability?
3. Have you ever mourned personal hurts? If not, why not? What would you need from "meaningful others" in your life to help you mourn?

Suggestions for Practical Application

1. Using Chart # 6 on page 72, write down those who have offended you. Have you forgiven them? Reread the suggestions about forgiveness on pages 66-69 and pray about your response to your offenders.
2. Using Chart # 6 on page 72, list your needs that are currently being neglected. Reread the material on pages 63-66 and work through the three steps of action.
3. Undoubtedly, you have at times neglected meeting the needs of your family members and friends. Using Chart # 7 on page 73, list those who you have neglected, the

specific ways you have neglected them. Then reread pages 66-69 and develop a plan to correct the offense through confession, forgiveness, and repentance.

Chart # 6 - Dealing with unmet needs

These people have offended me in the past. Here is my response.

Offender - _____

Offense - _____

My response - _____

Offender - _____

Offense - _____

My response - _____

Offender - _____

Offense - _____

My response - _____

I feel that these principle care-givers are neglecting my needs. Here is my plan of action.

Principle care-giver - _____

My needs which are being neglected - _____

_____

My plan of action - _____

_____

Principle care-giver - _____

My needs which are being neglected - _____

_____

My plan of action - _____

_____

Chart # 7 - Accepting responsibility for people I have neglected

Because we are all imperfect humans living in an imperfect world, it is inevitable that we will at times neglect and offend those whom God has called us to give to. These offenses must be Scripturally corrected. List those whom you have offended, name the offense, and establish a plan to correct the situation.

I have neglected/offended _____
How I have neglected/offended them _____

_____

How I plan to make restitution _____

_____

I have neglected/offended _____
How I have neglected/offended them _____

_____

How I plan to make restitution _____

_____

I have neglected/offended _____
How I have neglected/offended them _____

_____

How I plan to make restitution _____

_____

Appendix A

Maintaining Healthy Relationships... Dealing With Conflict

Healthy relationships need constant attention. We often think that only bad relationships need attention, but actually the best relationships are those that are constantly worked on and "fine tuned." All types of relationships - husband/wife, friendships, employer/employee, parent/child - will benefit from the following scriptural principles that teach us how to keep relationships healthy and current.

"Do not let the sun go down while you are still angry" (Ephesians 4:26).

The first principle is: deal immediately with misunderstandings, hurts, and anything else that would cause you to be angry. This Scripture suggests that anger should not be internalized. Unresolved hurt may lead to negative emotions such as bitterness, fear, guilt, condemnation, and despair; and these may eventually affect us in physiological ways such as insomnia, high bloodpressure, anxiety, or headaches. Since there are no "perfect relationships," all relationships will inevitably produce hurts, and our reluctance to deal with them promptly causes us to internalize negative emotions that God never intended for us to bear.

"Speak the truth in love" (Ephesians 4:15).

The second principle is: deal with conflicts by sharing truth and always share the truth motivated by love.

First, this verse tells us *what* to speak - the truth. Whenever there's a conflict in interpersonal relationships, seek the truth. Many times we're upset over something we're misinformed about. Often, just talking out a situation - getting the facts - will dissolve many conflicts. Proverbs 18:17 says, *"The first to present his case seems right, till another comes forward and questions him."* Which simply means - there's always two sides to every story.

But this verse also speaks about *how* the truth should be spoken, how it should be delivered. Armed with the truth, you can't act like a "007 agent" with a license to kill, using the truth to maim and hurt; you must minister the truth *in love.* The Bible won't let you go up to someone in a crowd and blurt out, "You're overweight," even though it may be the truth, because you'd be in violation of the "in love" clause.

If we ignore either admonition in this verse, we'll become either a "hider" or a "hurler." "Hiders" don't share the truth; "hurlers" share the truth - but not in love. Both approaches produce disastrous results. "Healers" share the truth in love.

"A gentle answer turns away wrath, but a harsh word stirs up anger" (Proverbs 15:1).

The third principle is: learn to diffuse volatile conversations by speaking gentle words. What happens if you're verbally attacked by someone who hasn't memorized Ephesians 4:15? How do you respond to a "hurler"? The answer is not to hurl back, for then you fall into the trap of "returning insult for insult," a battle in which there is no winner.

What will neutralize anger? A gentle answer. What does a gentle answer sound like? Here are some examples: "I'm sorry this situation has disappointed you. Let's talk about it." "I want to do everything I can to restore peace to this relationship. Let's talk." "If I've done something to offend you, I want to know about it so I can make it right."

Speaking a gentle answer doesn't mean you have to eat crow; it's not an open invitation for verbal abuse. Nor does it mean that someone can come "dump on you," then walk off, leaving you frustrated and confused. This verse is best applied to the first 90 seconds of a volatile conversation; it will diffuse an explosive situation before it gets out of hand. Once the conversation is manageable, then reconciliation is possible.

This week, see how often you can apply these three verses as you seek to maintain healthy relationships.

"Maintaining Healthy Relationships" is taken from the June, 1994 issue of **The Marriage and Family Intimacy Newsletter**.   For a free 5-month gift subscription to the monthly newsletter, call or write the CMFI office.

The Center For Marriage and Family Intimacy
P.O.Box 201808, Austin, Texas 78720-1808
1-800-881-8008 Fax 512-795-0853